PUBLIC POLICY

AN OVERVIEW OF APPROACHES TO THE STUDY OF PUBLIC POLICY

AJAY VAID

"To all of those who encouraged me to pursue my dreams and all my wonderful readers"

Contents

Preface

Many theories, models, and approaches for analyzing policy-making have been developed by political and social scientists. The theoretical approaches include elite theory, group theory, political systems theory and institutionalism, policy output analysis, incremental theory, and rational-choice theory, all of which are primarily concerned with public policy-making as a process. As a result, this work attempts to examine each theory, highlighting its strengths and limitations. Each of the theories discussed, when applied skillfully and selectively, can contribute to a better understanding of policymaking.

Acknowledgements

I am overjoyed to be able to place this work in the hands of my esteemed readers. I owe a huge debt of gratitude to the intellectuals whose ideas I had the honour of quoting. The goal of the work is to make the students understand the various approaches to the study of public policy. If any reader points out a flaw in the book, I will be grateful and do my best to fix it in the next edition. Suggestions that are beneficial will be greatly appreciated. Please e-mail ajayvaid73@gmail.com with your valuable comments.

Aside from that, I'd like to thank the Publisher (NOTION PRESS), who has gone to great lengths to get the book out as soon as possible and without any printing errors. Finally, I did like to express my heartfelt gratitude to Prof. D.R SINGH and MS NIRLAPE KOUR (ASSISTANT PROFESSOR), who encouraged me to write and greatly helped me in gathering reliable information and sources.

AJAY VAID

Prologue

Public policy was once a rule of law handed down by monarchs and aristocrats. Years of discussion, debate and even war have revealed the evolution toward a negotiated approach to public policy. Many major historic public policy documents helped shape the modern approach to policy creation. Several documents, including the Magna Carta and the United States Constitution, demonstrate how the world evolved toward modern ideals. Almost anything, including major wars, can be altered by public policy. The United States participation in World War I and World War II reflected a dramatic shift in U.S. public policy, indicating an expansion of U.S. policy influence. The expansion of people's and government's power marks the evolution of public policy. Public policy leaders have contributed to the approaches seen in modern government throughout history. Every day, history is made. People who earn a master's degree in public administration and policy gain the knowledge and experience needed to analyze and manage local and global policies. In general, public policy refers to a government's actions (plans, laws, and behaviors). Concerns about new governance draw attention to the extent to which these actions are now frequently performed by state agents rather than directly by the state. Public policy exists to influence how other important decisions are made, and it is typically formed in response to a specific issue of public interest. Public policy is supposed to provide a solution to a problem. Effective public policy will strengthen democratic institutions and processes, serve justice, promote empathetic and active citizenship, and solve problems efficiently and effectively without causing a political schism. The important role of public policy is to make society live a better life and to significantly maintain the delivery of goods and services. It is regarded as a mechanism for developing an economic-social system, a procedure for determining the future, and so on. Public policy analysis entails assessing issues of public importance with the goal of providing facts and statistics about the scope and impact of the government's various policies. The primary goal of public policy analysis is to determine the extent to which policies achieve their objectives. It is evident that the area of public policy has an important role in the public domain, it can upsurge the growing density of the society. Public policy is not only worried about the explanation and extension of the reasons and concerns of the government actions. It also has the development of scientific information about the services determining public policy. The examination of public policy aids us in determining the social ills of the matter under the examination. Policies do more than effect alteration in the situations of the society, they bring the people together to follow the uniformity in the state. These public policies are the main devices for any democratic nation and they improve the social and economic procedures from the present to the future. Hence, the examination of public policy has become a significant element of the academic society as well.

CHAPTER ONE

PUBLIC POLICY: MEANING, NATURE, SCOPE, AND IMPORTANCE

Introduction: The lives of the citizens everywhere are formed by public policies, whether we are aware of them or not. The dream of improved life while its achievement rests on our efforts, will probably contain public policies to aid the result of it. Public policy is a subject or field of inquiry that has a long past, though the current public policy analysis has a specific American and 20th-century fragrance. The public policy seeds were sown in the 1940s and made a significant influence on the government and academic organizations over these years. In the early 1950s public policy developed as an academic search and from then it has been securing new measurements and is stressed tough to attain the position of a discipline in the area of Social science. As a study of „products" of government, policy forms a significant component in many courses and academic programs in various disciplines like political science, public administration, economics, and business management.

Definitions of Public Policy:

Dye, says that...institutional studies usually described specific government institutions...without systematically inquiring about the impact of institutional characteristics on policy outputs...However, the linkage between institutional arrangements and the content of policy remained largely unexamined. The definitions of public policy are as follows:

Thomas Dye defines public policy as "whatever governments choose to do or not to do".

Dimock stated public policy as "deciding at any time or place what objectives and substantive measures should be chosen in order to deal with a particular problem".

Chandler and Plano, define public policy as "the strategic use of resources to alleviate national problems or governmental concerns".

Freeman and Sherwoods stated that it is the public answer to the interest in refining human circumstances. In these definitions, there is a deviation between what governments agree to do and what they essentially do. Public policy is a controller which the government has planned for direction and practice in certain problem areas.

In the current times, the study of public policy has evolved into what is virtually a fresh branch of social sciences called, „policy sciences". In 1951, Harold Lasswell, for the first time, the concept of policy science was framed. Presently, the policy sciences have departed far away from immature ambitions for societally applicable information.

On the basis of the above-mentioned definitions of public policy, certain conclusions can be drawn:-

Firstly, public policy is a proposition or goal-oriented activity.

Secondly, policy consists of courses or patterns of actions by governmental officials. Non-governmental actors or factors may influence policy developments.

Thirdly, a policy is what governments actually do, not what they intend to do.

Fourthly, a public policy may be either positive or negative in form. Positively, it may involve some form of overall government action. Negatively, it involves a decision by the government not to take action in a particular direction.

To sum up, it can be said that public policy is a purposive course of action followed by an actor dealing with a problem or matter of concern.

Concept of Public and Policy:

In the literature of academics, the term „public policy is regularly utilized in our present-day life and we regularly refer to the policies which are implanted like, national, education policy, agriculture policy, health policy, wage policy so on. In fact, this is the area where the public is involved. The concept of public policy is assumed, that there is a domain of life which has totally individual and is not private, which is believed in collective.

The Notion of the Public:

It is very significant to recognize the notion of „public" for a discussion of „public policy". We regularly use the words such as „public interest", „public sector", „public opinion", „public health", and so on. The public policy has to do with which are labeled as the public, as contrasting to scopes concerning „private". The measurements of the public are usually mentioned as, „public ownership" or governor for „public purpose". The term public contains all the measurements of human action observed as needing governmental involvement or social directive. Though, there has been a battle between what is „public" and what is „private".

The Notion of Policy:

The notion of „public", and the idea of „policy" is also not exactly defined. Policy signifies, among other things, „guidance for action". It might take the procedure of

1. Commanding conclusion,
2. Principle or value
3. The purposive course of action,
4. Method of governance
5. Manifestation of considered judgment
6. Look at political rationality and
7. Declaration of common goals.

In a Machiavellian sense, the policy is the base of power. While bureaucracy derived its legitimacy from its claim to "State", the politician claimed that their authority rested on the approval of their policies by the electorates. Hogwood and Gunn specified ten usages of the word policy as

1. A label for the field of activity
2. An expression of the desired state of affairs
3. Specific proposals
4. The decision of governments
5. Formal authorization
6. A program
7. Output
8. Outcome
9. A theory or model

10. A process.

Meaning of Policy:

The meaning of the term „policy" is varying like other concepts of social science. Unluckily, the policy itself somewhat takes diverse procedures. David Easton defined policy as the „output" of the political system, and „public policy" as „the authoritative allocation of values for the whole society". The measures of this alteration in the methods of acceptance from other definitions progress by the scholars in this field.

Henry defines public policy as, "A script (course of action) adopted and pursued by the government". Anderson stated that policy is observed as a "Purposive course of action followed by an actor or set of actors in dealing with a problem or matter of concern". According to Sir, Geoffrey Vickers, policies are judgments giving way, unity, and steadiness to the course of the act for which the decision-making body is accountable.

Friedrich looks at policy as, ...a proposed course of action of a person, group, or government within a given environment providing obstacles and opportunities with the policy was proposed to utilized and overcome in an effort to reach a goal or realize an objective or purpose.

According to Parsons, who stated about it as "A policy is an attempt to define and structure a rational basis for action or inaction". In present terminology, a policy is broadly defined as a course of action or plan, a set of political purposes.

It might well be sufficiently defined "policy" as a purposive development of actions taken or accepted by those in power in chase of convinced goals or objectives. It must be added here that public policies are the policies accepted and executed by government bodies and officials. They are framed by what Easton appeals to the „authorities" in a political system. Namely, "elders, paramount chiefs, executives, legislators, judges, administrators, councilors, monarchs, and the like". He stated as, these are the persons who "engage in the daily affairs of a political system", are "recognized by most members of the system as having the responsibility for these matters" and take action that is "accepted and binding most of the time by most of the members so long as their actions within the limit of their roles".

Difference between Policy and Rules

The term policy is sometimes confused with terms like rules, customs, procedures, and so on. However, there is a fundamental difference between each of them. "Policy" is dynamic and flexible whereas "rule" is specific and rigid. Policies are usually broader than rules and are stated in more general language. Whereas policies serve as guides to action, rules specifically state what must or what may not be done. Rules are usually reinforced by specific, stated penalties, but policies allow room for variation in their use without entailing immediate, specific, and stipulated penalties.

Policy Differs from Customs, Decisions, and Plans

There is also a difference between policy and custom in so far as the former is the product of conscious effort, while the latter grows automatically in the soil of society. The policy should also be distinguished from the decision. Though policy in itself is a big decision, it provides the framework within which several other series of decisions are taken. The policy is also different from the procedure. The procedure exists to effectuate the policy. Procedures are actually established as the prescribed way of doing something. They become a standard method by which work is performed. The policy deals with basic issues, basic to the working of the whole administrative machinery. These issues may be simple and limited in nature or they may be complex and numerous. For simple issues, it will be easier to make decisions, for complicated issues, decisions may require considerable research, study, and analysis. Policies are sometimes also confused with plans, but both are quite different from each other. Policies are conceived as directives sent down as rules to be followed. Plans, on the other hand, are not easily perceived or communicated. Plans are transformed into policies often; however, the plan may not be known, although policies derived from it are clearly spelled out. The policies may in fact force the creation of an objective statement of the plan rather than being derived from it.

Nature of Public Policy:

It is very much evident that policy might take different procedures like legislation, executive orders, or official acts. They actually comprise of a set of intentions or objectives a combination of devices or means for the attainment of intentions, a description of governmental or non-governmental units indicted with the accountability of transporting out the intentions, and distribution of resources for the necessary tasks. To recognize a public policy, it is very much needed to examine its nature. A policy may contain specific or general, broad or narrow, simple or complex, public or private written or unwritten explicit or implicit, discretionary or detailed, and quantitative or qualitative.

Public policy is, in fact, kill because these tasks regularly some information about the social sciences, and in this case, the stress is on the „public policy" which is known as „government policy", selected by a government as a „direction for action". From the perspective of public policies, actions of government could be put broadly into two groups and they are:

1. Definite or Specific policies and

2. General, vague and inconsistent policies.

In reality, a government rarely will have a fixed of supervisory values for all its actions and in fact, the significant public policies are frequently made more clear specifically where the issue of law, regulation, or strategy is involved. The Supreme Court can give its decisions, by new interpretations to some of the articles of the Constitution which can be developed into the new policy.

These policies may be too unclear or too broad and may not be reliable to each other, in turbulent atmospheres like the current ones government has to make regular actions without reference to any particular policy, sometimes government announces some sort of policy for political convenience or for some reasons, in such cases, the government will not have any intention to carry it successfully. Hence, it is likely to have a policy without action or it can have action without policy. Public policies are alive only in a set of practices and precedents. The public policies are embodied only in an unwritten Constitution of the United Kingdom is the best instance of this form of public policy.

The public policy contains a major segment of actions, like, development policy, economic growth, socio-economic growth, equality, social justice, or any other such policy that may be accepted by national policy. Hence, it can be observed a single policy in various written documents, it may be narrow, covering a particular action, like family planning which is reserved to a certain division of the people or it can be for an extensive range of people in the country, for instance, the government can accept that no child is adult unless he attains the age of 16 years (recent amendment). Public policy is an area commonly defined by policy areas like health, education, housing, economic, environmental, transport, and social and it is mostly set that interdisciplinary and intergovernmental relations taking place. These policies can be developed either by the central government or state government or sometimes „mega policies" act as a kind of master policy. The word mega policy is coined by Yehezkel Dror. The broad policies which are an expression of national aims are the instances for the mega policies, eg. Economic growth, social justice, etc.

It is very much important to understand the nature of the policy means, it must contain an objective, an aim or a goal, or a purpose because a policy is a guide for action. In fact, all the mega policies are purposive and are object-oriented but it is conceivable that a government can have a policy without any recognizable objectives or purpose. It can accept any policy without any particular goals. The significance regarding the goals and objectives is that, while studying the policies of government collective as a total, the multidimensional nature of goals and objectives, as well as the presence of several irregularities and even ambiguities becomes observable. Government can accept vague, inconsistent, or even contradictory policies so that to gratify all the pressure groups and political parties.

The public policy can be a positive or negative one, in its positive form, it can contain some system of evident government activity to treat a specific problem. Whereas, in the negative form, it might contain a decision by a public servant not to take action on some sort of matter on which the government action is required. These policies sometimes will have legally coercive so that people can adopt them legally for instance all the people will pay the taxes in order to stay away from the fines. These public policies make public organizations different from private organizations.

Scope of the Public Policy:

It is a noteworthy discipline examination and practice, meanwhile, the appearance of public policy as a field of investigation has extended in theoretical scope and application. A noteworthy amount of the study of public policy contains the growth of situations of current styles. In several developing countries, there is an excessive burden on the governments to speed up the growth of the nation, make usage of modern and applicable technological inventions, accept and enable essential institutional alterations, upsurge the production of the nation, make total usage of human and other sources, and advance the level of living standards. These tendencies and growths have hence, improved both the magnitude and possibility of the public policy. Michael Teitz pronounces the outreach of public policy in terms of the citizen's life cycle as follows:

"Modern urban man is born in a publicly financed hospital, receives his education in a publically supported school and university, spends a good part of his time traveling on publically built transport facilities, communicate by the post offices or quasi-public telephone system, drinks his public drinking water, disposes of his garbage through a public removal system, reads his library books, picnics in his public parks, is protected by public police, fire, and health systems. Ideological conservatives notwithstanding his daily life are inextricably bound up with government decisions on these various public services".

The public policy stresses the problems of the public, according to Heidenheimer, public policy is the study of "how, why and what effect governments pursue particular courses of action and inaction". Dye stated about it as, "what government does, why they do it, and what difference it makes".

According to Lasswell, policy orientation is a multi-method, multi-disciplinary, problem that emphasizes worried to plan the context of the policy procedure.

Objectives of Public Policy

A public policy may have either a micro or macro perspective. The micro policy is designed for a specific or a local area but a macro policy has a far wider application. It may be employed in the whole polity or the whole economy. It may be noted that macroeconomic or macro-political policy objectives are bound to have many common grounds. Needless to add that an economic policy is an important part of public policy. Thus a public policy will essentially incorporate many economic items and desiderata. Public policy involves the manipulation of different social- economic-political variables like taxation, price level, income, employment, public expenditure, money supply, and so forth. There are many policy variables in which policymakers are ultimately interested; for example, employment, price stability, economic growth, the balance of payment equilibrium, and so on. The main macro policy variables or the objectives of the public policy are (i) Price stability (ii) Generation of maximum employment (iii) Economic growth (iv) Income equality and (v) Balance of payment equilibrium.

The objectives may also be framed in terms of macro-political considerations. In such cases, the objectives of public policy can be said to be secularism, equilibrium, maximum freedom and liberty, equality before the law, social justice, and so on. The policymakers must classify the objectives into short-term and long-term keeping in mind the immediate and distant social-economic desiderata. The short-term goals should be tried to realize first. But short-term public objectives should not serve as a constraint for the long-term objectives. For instance, price stability is a short-term objective whereas economic growth is a long-term objective. No measure intended to achieve price stability should disturb the long-term objective of capital formation and economic growth.

The meaning and nature of public policy will become more clear by throwing light on different characteristics of public policy. Some of the major characteristics of public policymaking are:

Public Policy Making is a Very Complex Process: Policymaking involves many components which are interconnected by communication and feedback loops and which interact in different ways. Some parts of the process are explicit and directly observable, but many others proceed through hidden channels that the officials themselves are often only partly aware of. These hidden procedures are very difficult, and often impossible to observe. Thus guidelines are often formed by a series of single decisions that result in a 'policy' without any one of the decision-makers being aware of that process.

It is a Dynamic Process: Policymaking is a process, that is a continuing activity taking place within a structure; for sustenance, it requires a continuing input of resources and motivation. It is a dynamic process, which changes with time, the sequences of others, its sub-processes, and phases vary internally and with respect to each other.

Policymaking Comprises Various Components: The complexity of public policy-making as we know is an important characteristic of policymaking. Public policy formulation often involves a great variety of substructures. The identity of these substructures and the degree of their involvement in policy-making, vary because of different issues, circumstances, and societal values.

Policy Structure makes Different Contributions: This characteristic suggests that every substructure makes a difference, and is sometimes a unique contribution to public policy. What sort of contribution substructures make, depends in part on their formal and informal characteristics which vary from society to society.

Decision-Making: Policymaking is a species of decision-making because it lets us use decision-making models for dealing with policymaking.

Lays down Major Guidelines: Public policy, in most cases, lays down general - directives, rather than detailed instructions, on the main lines of action to be followed. After main lines of action have been decided on, detailed sub-policies that translate the general theory into more concrete terms are usually needed to execute it.

Results in Action: Decision-making can result in action in changes in the decision-making itself, or both or neither. The policies of most socially significant decision-making, such as most public policymaking are intended to result in action. Also, policies directed at the policymaking apparatus itself such as efficiency drives in government are action-oriented.

Directed at the Future: Policymaking is directed at the future. This is one of its most important characteristics since it introduces the ever-present elements of uncertainty and a doubtful prediction that establish the basic tone of nearly all policymaking. Actual policymaking tends to formulate policies in vague and elastic terms; because the future is so uncertain. It permits policymakers to adjust their policy according to emerging facts and enables them to guard against unforeseen circumstances.

Mainly Formulated by Governmental Organs: Public policy is also directed in part, at private persons and non-governmental structures, as 'when it calls for a law prohibiting a certain type of behavior or appeals to citizens to engage in private saving. But public policy, in most cases, is primarily directed at governmental organs, and only intermediately and secondarily at other factors.

Aims at Achieving what is in the Public Interest: However difficult it might be to find out what the "public interest" may completely refer to, the term never the less conveys the idea of "general" orientation and seems, therefore to be important and significant. Furthermore, there is good evidence that the image of "public interest" influences the public policymaking process and is therefore at least, as conceived by the various public policymaking units, a "real" phenomenon, and an important operational tool for the study of policymaking.

Use of Best Possible Means: In abstract terminology, public policy-making aims at achieving the maximum net benefit. Benefits and costs take in part the form of 8 realized values and impaired values, respectively, and cannot in most cases be expressed in commensurable units. Often, quantitative techniques can therefore dot public policy: be used in this area of public policymaking but neither the qualitative significance Meaning and Nature of maximum net benefits as an aim nor the necessity to think broadly about alternative public policies in terms of benefits and costs are therefore reduced.

Involvement of Various Bodies/Agencies: Industrial workers, voters, .intellectuals; legislators, bureaucrats, political parties, political executives, judiciary- etc. are the various organs that participate in public policymaking and can influence the policy process to a great extent.

Importance of Public Policy:

It is evident that public policy is a significant factor in the democratic government and it emphasizes the public and its problems, in fact, it is a discipline that is branded as public. The concept of public policy assumes that there is an area of life that is totally individual but said in public. Likewise, public policies have a significant purpose to work in a society where democracy prevails. The important role of the public policy is to make the society lead a better life and to maintain the delivery of the goods and services are significant, it is regarded as the mechanism for developing an economic-social system, a procedure for determining the future, and so on.

BASIS OF POLICY FORMULATION

Policy, from whatever source - legislature or administration -it may emanate, must be based on factual data and accurate information. To the legislature, it is the administration which supplies the necessary information but where the administration obtains that information. Broadly speaking, there are four ways through which administration collects the necessary information :

(i) Internal Sources: Every department is a center to which flow periodic reports, returns, statements, accounts, and various other material from various field establishments. These reports and other material are recorded by the department for future use whenever the need arises. Some departments employ special agencies for the collection of data in certain special fields. Several Ministries in India have made special arrangements and established special machinery for the collection of statistics and data helpful for policy-making. The Central Statistical Organization, the National Sample Survey, The Bureau of Public Enterprises, the Directorate of Industrial Statistics, and various other organizations are working for the collection of information and statistics. The data so collected are properly processed, organized, and interpreted to reveal certain facts essential for policy-making.

(2) External Sources: To supplement the internal data which may be insufficient, the administration takes to collecting information from external sources. It establishes contacts with private bodies, unions, associations, chambers, etc., in order to get a true picture of facts. Internal information is likely to be biased and hence inaccurate and unreliable because it travels through the official channels and the agency reporting it may not like to reveal all that is the fact. In our country, the government does consult and tries to know the essence of public opinion through various labor unions, chambers of commerce, and other professional associations. Before a Five Year Plan is actually approved, the draft outline is thrown open for discussion to various bodies all over the country. The suggestions received are duly considered and incorporated, where approved, in working out the final Plan.

(3) Special Investigatons : Special investigations may be conducted by the appointment of Commissions and

Committees of inquiry for finding facts in respect of a particular matter or field. Such investigations are very useful for policy-making as they provide the maximum thought in a particular field. Examples of such Commissions/Committees are numerous both in our country and abroad. The Royal Commissions appointed from time to time in England, the Hoover Commission in the USA, the Central Pay Commissions, the Universities Radhakrishnan Commission, the Local Finance Enquiry Commission, the Secondary Education Commission, the Press Commission, the Taxation Commission, Sarkaria Commission on Central-State relations, etc. in India are the examples of special investigating bodies. These Commissions have specific terms of reference, they examine witnesses, both official and non-official and obtain facts and views which they convey to the Government in the form of recommendations. These recommendations serve as the basis for policy-making and effecting reforms.

(4) Research and Study: Research and studies may be organized by the Government and non-official agencies to discover certain facts and views. Administrative research may be conducted by such bodies as the Division of Administrative Management in the Office of Management and Budget in the USA, O & M in the Treasury, and in various other departments in U. K. Organisation and Methods Division in the Cabinet Secretariat with its cells in other departments in India. Similarly, non-official bodies like Brooking Institution, The Public Administration Clearing House in the USA, the British Institute of Public Administration, and the Indian Institute of Public Administration also conduct research and provide facts for policy formulation Technical research and study may be conducted by technical institutions set up for the purpose. The Geological, Botanical, Zoological Survey in India, the Council of Scientific and Industrial Research, various laboratories electro-chemicals, metallurgy, mining, the Atomic Energy devoted to research in building techniques, drugs, food, technology,

Commissions, the Oil and Natural Gas Commission, etc., are some examples of Institutions engaged in research. Every modern government, anxious as it is to make improvements, has to depend on these research bodies for the mine of information and facts they supply. Every new policy must take cognizance of the new research and material provided by these bodies. The governments are also obliged to take the help of some international agencies such as the United Nations and its affiliates, World Health Organisation, International Labour Organisation, International Bank for Reconstruction and Development, International Monetary Fund, Commonwealth Secretariat, etc. Of late, the policy-making organizations have been seeking inputs from the world trade bodies and regional blocks such as the World Trade Organisation, Association of Southeast Asian Nations (ASEAN) South Asian Association for Regional Corporation (SAARC), etc.

Other Factors Influencing Policy-Making

Policies are not made in a "vacuum". That is to say that policymakers must take cognizance of various factors in formulating policies. They cannot act arbitrarily, more so in a democratic country. First, every policy must be in consonance with the provisions of the constitution (as interpreted by the law courts) and the laws made by the legislature. Secondly, every policy must take into account the prevailing customs, traditions, and conventions of the people. That is to say that a policy must not be against established ways of life of the people unless it is extremely desirable to frame one for banning a social evil. Thirdly, a policy must take into consideration International law and world opinion for no country can live an isolated life. International law is constantly becoming important and every member living in the family of nations must play the game according to the rules. Fourthly, if a policy of a department affects the policy of some other department or organization, the department framing the policy must have prior consultations with the department affected. Such a clearance is very important for the homogeneity of administration. Finally, a policy must be framed after due consultation with the persons or groups of persons, their unions and associations, and other interests likely to be affected by the policy for this would help the policy-maker to analyze the difficulties likely to be faced in the execution of the policy.

Thus policies have to take into consideration several factors. In the words of Seckler Hudson: "Policies are arrived at, then, in all sorts of ways, conditioned by all sorts of matters. The various organizations that participate indirectly or directly in policy formulation are the legislature, the executive, the judiciary through interpretations and judge-made laws, top administrators, political parties, pressure groups, people, etc. Policy-making is a continuous process. Although it may seem to be a decision of a particular body or department, in practice, however, the process is widespread although the organization and the particular body announcing it is the last link of a long chain of the previous history of the matter. It is, therefore, a collective activity, a cooperative endeavor, and an effort in which many people participate.

Gladden distinguishes four different levels in policy-making:(a) political or general policy framed by the Parliament, (b) executive policy framed by the Cabinet, (c) administrative policy that is, the form in which the administrator works out the will of the Government, and (d) technical policy, that is, the day-to-day policy adopted by the officials in carrying out the administrative policy.

The Public Policy Process

Public policy involves an interactive and dynamic process and is never a one-time event. In most cases, public policy deals with the rules and directives associated. It comprises a sub-policy that includes the exact details about the policy, together with the concerned implementation techniques.

There are five main steps involved in the public policy process include following:

- Identification of the Problem
- Formulation of Policy
- Adaption of Policy
- Implementation of Policy
- Evaluation of Policy

In a nutshell, formulating, implementing, and following public policies helps to regulate and rectify the operations of governance. Every institution needs to have its own set of rules and regulations, Public Policy, and laws to hold everything in place.

Types of public policy

Public policies are the collective actions taken by the government, and it includes law, rules, regulations, case studies, judgments, and government programs. Public policy can be categorized into the following main types.

Distributive

These policies render goods and services to the members of an institution or an organization and also distribute their costs among these members. Distributive policies are concerned with certain segments of society and benefit large groups. It is associated with the public welfare, transfer of goods and services, public education, health services, public safety, highways, and the like. In other words, distributive policies encompass all public welfare and assistance programs. Some more examples of distributive policies are adult education programs, food relief, social insurance, vaccination camps, etc.

Regulatory

The regulatory policies and practices involved with public policy strive to regulate and control multiple economic sectors of the state or the concerned institution. Regulatory policies are formulated to keep a check on the tendencies of the institution to divert from the established plans and schemes as declared by the government. These policies are concerned with the regulation of business, trade, safety measures, public utilities, and others. Independent institutions or organizations do it on behalf of the government. Regulatory policies compel specific types of behavior and limit the discretion of agencies or individuals. The limitation of the highway speed limit is an excellent example of the regulatory policies implemented by the government. These policies define and reward good behavior and punish and condemn the bad ones through fines or sanctions.

Regulatory policies are concerned with the regulation of trade, business, safety measures, public utilities, etc. This type of regulation is done by independent organizations that work on behalf of the government. In India, we have Life Insurance Corporation, Reserve Bank of India,

Hindustan Steel, State Electricity Boards. State Transport Corporations, State Financial Corporations, etc., which are engaged in regulatory activities. The policies made by the government, pertaining to these services and organizations rendering these services are known as regulatory policies.

Redistributive

Policies are dynamic and ever-changing. There is nothing called static laws. So one needs to create a blueprint and implement them appropriately. However, one also needs to be prepared for some unexpected results. Social policies are subject to changes in either the initial stages of implementation or at the legislative or decision-making stages. These are associated with the rearrangement of policies that is concerned with bringing about specific changes in the economic and social status of the state or the institution. Redistributive policies are concerned with the rearrangement of policies that are concerned with bringing about basic social and economic changes. Certain public goods and welfare services are disproportionately divided among certain segments of society, these goods and service5 are streamlined through redistributive policies.

Substantive

These policies are concerned with the general welfare and development of the society, the programs like the provision of education and employment opportunities, economic stabilization, law and order enforcement, anti-pollution legislation, etc. are the result of substantive policy formulation. These policies have vast areas of operation affecting the general welfare and development of society as a whole. These do not relate to any particular or privileged segments of society. Such policies have to be formulated keeping in view the prime character of the constitution's socio-economic problems and the level of moral claims of the society.

Substantive policies focus on those sectors of the society or economy which are affected by various public policies like educational policies, agricultural policies, urban policies, health policies, defense policies, and many more. These policies are not generally related to particular segments of society.

Capitalization

Under the capitalization policies, the Union government provides financial subsidies to the local and state governments, such subsidies are also granted to the central and state business undertakings or some other important sphere if necessary. Capitalization policies are different in nature from the substantive, regulatory, distributive, and redistributive policies as no provision for public welfare services is made through these.

Constituent

Constituent policies deal with laws and create executive power entities. They also deal with fiscal policies under certain circumstances.

Technical Public Policy

It relates to the policies framed for the arrangement of procedures, rules, and framework which a system shall provide for the discharge of action by various agencies on the field.

Relevance of Policy Making in Public Administration

Policymaking is of supreme significance and relevance in Public Administration. Appleby is of the view that the essence of Public Administration is policymaking. "Policy is prior to every action. The policy sets the task for administration Policy is in fact Planning for action; it is getting ready for setting the sails to reach the desired destination.

Ever since Wilson wrote his essay in "The Study of Administration" published in 1887, the politics-administration dichotomy school of thought tended to regard policy as outside the scope of administration. In the words of Wilson, "The field of administration is a field of business. It is removed from the hurry and strife of politics". Wilson was followed by Goodnow and as late as 1926, L. D. White drew a distinction between administration and politics.

It is now being increasingly realized that the politics-administration dichotomy cannot work and that administration cannot be completely divorced from policy-making. Luther Gulick was one of the first advocates of this view. To quote Appleby "Administrators are continually laying down rules for the future, and administrators are continually determining what the law is, what it means in terms of action, what the rights of parties are with respect both to transactions in process and transactions in prospect.....Administrators also participate in another way in the making of policy for the future; they formulate recommendations for legislation, and this is a part of the function of policy-making." Public officials are associated with policy formulation in three important ways. First, they have to supply facts, data, and criticism as to the workability of policy to the Ministers or to the legislature if the initiative for policymaking comes from them. The members of the legislature or the Ministers are amateurs who have risen to positions because of the popular will and not because of administrative talent and as such, they have to give due weight to the suggestions of the officials. Secondly, in many cases, the initiative for the policy or legislation emanates from the administration. This is because of the fact that it is the administration that is in constant touch with the general public and is in a better position to understand the difficulties that arise in the execution of legislation. It has, therefore, to make suggestions and formulate proposals for removing those difficulties and in the process, it may have to, if need be, ask for amendments in the existing law or even for more laws. In such cases, policy proposals emanating from the administration and legislature only put their seal of approval on them. Thirdly, on account of lack of time and knowledge, the legislature passes skeleton Acts and leaves the details to the administration. It is here that Administration is most supreme in policy-making. In order to execute these Acts, the administration frames rules, regulations, and by-laws which is a major contribution to policy-making.

Conclusion:

It is evident that the area of public policy has an important role in the public domain, it can upsurge the growing density of the society. Public policy is not only worried about the explanation and extension of the reasons and concerns of the government actions. It also has the development of scientific information about the services determining public policy. The examination of public policy aids us in determining the social ills of the matter under the examination. Policies do more than effect alteration in the situations of the society, they bring the people together to follow the uniformity in the state. These public policies are the main devices for any democratic nation and they improve the social and economic procedures from the present to the future. Hence, the examination of public policy has become a significant element of the academic society as well.

CHAPTER TWO

APPROACHES TO THE STUDY OF PUBLIC POLICY

Many theories, models, and approaches for analyzing policy-making have been developed by political and social scientists. The theoretical approaches include elite theory, group theory, political systems theory and institutionalism, policy output analysis, incremental theory, and rational-choice theory, all of which are primarily concerned with public policy-making as a process. The model formulated by Max Weber, a German sociologist, of relational imperative in making decisions which contain the starting point for the analysis of rationality in public policy. The other model is the incremental model, which was designed by Charles Lindblom, in the form of „incrementalism", the article was published in 1959, titled „The science of muddling through". It is actually, identified in the development of public policy methods. The model of the Mixed Scanning method was, developed by Amitai Etzioni, it is actually an altered model of the rational model policy.

As a result, this work attempts to examine each theory, highlighting its strengths and limitations. Each of the theories discussed, when applied skillfully and selectively, can contribute to a better understanding of policymaking.

Rational–Choice Theory

Rational–Choice Theory:

The rational-choice theory, which is sometimes called social-choice, public-choice, or formal theory, originated with economists and involves applying the principles of microeconomic theory to the analysis and explanation of political behavior (or nonmarket decision-making). It has now gained quite a few adherents among political scientists (Anderson, 1997). The perception of rationality stresses that the making of public policy is a selection amongst substitutes on a rational base. According to Dror, rational policymaking is "to choose the one best opinion". According to Robert Henry Haveman, it is designed to maximize "net value achievement". At the same time, „rationality" with „efficiency" when he said that, "a policy is rational when the difference between the values it achieves and the values it sacrifices is positive and greater than any other policy alternatives". He also stated that the notion of rationalism includes, "the calculation of all social, political, and economic values sacrificed or achieved by a public policy, not just those that can be measured in dollars".

Desires for Rational Analysis:

To choose a rational policy the policy formulators must be rational but, to be rational is not easy this was stated by Robert L. Lineberry. If one want to be rational it is likely to have:

1. Recognition and determination of objects

2. Grading of objects according to the significance

3. Recognition of likely policy substitutes for attaining those objectives

4. Cost-benefit analysis of policy substitutes

Dror also stated some of the needs for the sake of policy formulators in choosing a rational policy they should:

1. Understand all the value preferences and the comparative burdens of society.

2. Understand all the substitutes of the policy available

3. Understand all the outcomes of every substitute of the policy

4. Calculate the ratio of welfare to the cost of every policy substitute

5. Choose the best effective substitute policy

Framework for a Rational Man:

This rational model was stated by Lindblom, as the one which is utilized by a rational man who is met with the given difficulty. A rational man first clarifies his objectives, values, or goals and then positions or otherwise arranges them in his mind. After that the person will catalog all the significant conceivable methods of policies for attaining his objectives and examines all the essential outcomes that will follow from every substitute policies at such fact to equate outcomes of every policy with objects. Hence, the rational man must select the policy with outcomes utmost carefully equivalent to his objectives. In the procedure of rational decision making, instead of making an "ideal" decision, as stated by Simon, policy formulators break the complexity of the difficulties into small and known segments, select one choice which will be the best and gratifying, and evade needless indecision. This means that "Although individuals are intensely rational, their rationality is bounded by limited cognitive and emotional capacities".

Phases for Analysis of Rationality in Policy:

Rational Public policy formulation, hence, needs making tough options amongst policy substitutes. It involves many phases, like the following ones.

1. The rationality undertakes that, the maker of the policy must recognize the fundamental difficulty. He makes and fixes the priorities of the aim. It is very much required due to, one aim may be more significant than the other one.

2. As the second phase, the rational policymaker recognizes the kind of policy substitutes and choices that may obtain some of the aims. After that, he makes a total set of substitute policies and resources with burdens. The procedure of recognizing policy substitutes is of crucial significance, as it touches both the kind and quality of

substitutes.

3. The third phase needs the calculation of forecasts about the cost welfares of the policy substitutes. The ration policy formulator is needed to calculate for every policy substitute, both the anticipation that it would attain the target and also its cost. Therefore, here there is a question of calculation of the "cost payoff ratios of every substitute.

4. At the same time, with calculating net anticipation for every substitute, the rational policy formulator is needed to equate the substitutes with the maximum benefits, it is likely that the relating two substitutes, one might derive two times the benefits at the lowest cost.

5. The final phase is, choosing the utmost proficient policy substitute. If the rational policymaker has completed his job correctly the policy option must be straightforward.

When a policy option is executed, the rational policy formulator is needed to monitor this execution methodically, to know the accuracy of the anticipated estimations. The policy formulators would attempt to fill the excuses, in the policy or offer it up overall. This is called the feedback phase" of rational policymaking. The concept of rationality is espoused to such an extent that many kinds of rational decision models are to be found in the literature of social sciences was stated by, L.L. Wade and R.L. Curry. The instance of the rational method to a decision method that facilities rationality in policymaking has been given by Dye.

Restriction of the Rational Method:

The analysis of rationality in public policy is a problematic job. It suffers from many restrictions, in this regard, Simon states about it as, "It is impossible for the behavior of a single, isolated individual to reach any high degree of rationality". The concept of rationality is mentioned about so much and so comprehensively, that it impends to lose its meaning. It is more extensively backed than practiced. Let us converse some of the significant restraints to rational policymaking in the following sections.

Achieving Objects: This rational policy-making is a very problematic job, the anticipation of a rational policy to develop is all the time very bleak. It is due to the fact that, when the policy formulator suggests a rational policy, the difficulty is the query becomes so multifaceted that rational preparations become decisions that are made on the grounds of social goals. As an alternative, the maker of the policy only attempts to exploit his own rewards, like power, status, money, and re-election.

In acquiring Optimization: The rational policymaking model is anticipated to develop optimal outcomes, but in fact, it will not do every time. The public interest is taken to be more significant than being simply the total of personal interest in the policy. If air pollution control is regarded as public interest and it is due to each person sharing its benefits, then the tactic needed perhaps be that each automobile sold to be fitted with a costly set of anti-pollution emission control devices by making it more costly.

Conflict among Rational Choice and Need for Action: There is every time a conflict between rational hunt behavior and the need for action. As it was mentioned, policy formulators are not inspired to make decisions on the grounds of social objectives, but an attempt instead to exploit their own prizes, like power, status, and money. Second, the time for a comprehensive analysis of awaiting legislation perhaps be short. In an emergency condition, action is required straight away.

The Dilemma of Political Feasibility: The dilemma of political feasibility worries itself with what is likely. Feasibility of politics is intended according to Ralph Heitt, "the probability that, however, rational and desirable, a policy option would actually be adopted and implemented by the political system". Politicians frequently solve the dilemma of political feasibility by avoidance of conflict. Improbability about the outcomes of the diverse policy substitutes might force politicians to stick to earlier policies.

The Problem of Cost-Benefit Analysis: It is very problematic for the makers of the policy to calculate the cost-benefit ratios correctly when several varied social, economic, political, and cultural values are at stake. Separately from these, they also have personal requirements, hang-ups, and insufficiencies which make them incapable of rational decisions.

Nature and Environment Bureaucracy: The Other significant difficulty to rational policymaking is the environment of the bureaucracies. Dye opines: "The segmentalized nature of policymaking in large bureaucracies make it difficult to coordinate decision making so that the input of all of the various specialists is brought to where at the point of the decision". Segmentation of authority, gratifying aims, conflicting values, and restricted technology, improbability on the likely policy substitutes and outcomes thereof, and other aspects restrict the capability of the bureaucracies and other public institutions to make rational policies.

Incremental Model

Incremental Model:

This model was formulated by Charles Lindblom in 1959 and his method was a substitute for the customary rational model of decision making. According to him, the constraint of time, intelligence, and cost prevent policymakers from recognizing the full variety of policy substitutes and their outcomes. Charles Lindblom condemned the rational model and also disallowed the notion that the thinking in terms of phases or practical connections (supported by Lasswell and Easton) was of any factual value to the examination of policy procedure. It illustrated precisely the difference in terms of complete (or root) rationality supported by Simon and his own "successive limited comparisons" (or branch decision making). The comparison is as follows:

Comprehensive Rationality

1. Reorganization of social values or aims is needed for the empirical analysis of substitute politics

2. Policy formulation is come up to by the means-ends analysis

3. The test of a health policy is that it is a means to an accepted end

4. Analysis is complete including each related aspect

5. Theory is frequently heavily rested upon

Successive Limited Comparision (branch)

1. Choice of values or aims and empirical analysis of the required action are interconnected1. Choice of values or aims and empirical analysis of the required action are interconnected

2. Means ends analysis is frequently unfitting2. Means ends analysis is frequently unfitting

3. The test of a health policy is that several analysts recognize themselves directly accepting on a policy3. The test of a health policy is that several analysts recognize themselves directly accepting on a policy

4. Analysis is restricted4. Analysis is restricted

5. A successive restricted Comparision decreases on theory

The Incremental method (branch method) of making decisions includes the procedure of "continually building out from the current situation, step by step and by small degrees". In comparison the root method, as favored by the policy analysts, was to begin from "fundamentals a new each time, building on the past only on the experience embodied in a theory, and always prepared to start from the ground up". In 1979, Lindblom explained and enlarged upon his notion of incrementalism. As an analytical method, incrementalism includes "simple incremental analysis", which regards as substitutes only incremental alterations from present situations, "disjointed incrementalism", which employs "a mutually supporting set of simplifying and focusing strategies" comprising the division of analytical work to several members, and "strategic analysis" Lindblom suggests, that "successive limited comparison" is both applicable and truthful in such a situation of "bounded rationality".

Characteristics of Incremental Model: The following aspects are considered in the decision-making process:

1. Firstly, it ensues by a succession of incremental modifications. The makers of the policy adopt the legality of present policies due to the insecurity about the outcomes of fresh or dissimilar policies.

2. Secondly, it contains shared modifications and negotiations the exam of a healthy decision is treaty relatively than the object is attained. The Contract is reached very easily in policymaking when the item in disagreement rises or declines in budgets or alterations to present programs. Hence, incrementalism is important in decreasing political tension and upholding stability.

3. Thirdly, it contains, trial and error method, it is superior to a "futile attempt at superhuman comprehensiveness". Human beings seldom perform to exploit all their values; fairly, they perform to gratify specific demands. They rarely influence for "one best way", but as a substitute, search to find "a way what will

work". This search generally starts with the conversant-that is, with policy choices close to modern policies.

4. Fourthly, a policy is not formulated for one time, as Lane stated as "Incrementalism is thus more satisfactory from a theoretical point of view as it scores high on criteria like coherence and simplicity".

Simple Incremental Analysis:

In this type of analysis, those substitute policies or choices that are marginally diverse to the present policy are analyzed. Lindblom stated that „simple incremental analysis" is a fruitful procedure of continuing to create decisions. Supportive the significance of this device, Lindblom conserves: "Focusing on small variations from present policy... makes the most of available knowledge. Because the new options are not terribly different from the present and past policies a great deal of what administrators and other participants already know about existing programs will be applicable to evaluating the new proposals. While uncertainty may still be substantial, errors probably will be smaller".

Strategic Analysis:

Lindblom claims that since completeness of analysis is not possible because of several restraints, an analyst must take a middle position: "informed, thoughtful" usage of procedure to "simplify problems" so that to make healthy options. These procedures contain trial and error learning; systems analysis; operation research;

management by objects; program appraisal and assessment techniques. By the usage of these "informed and thoughtful" procedures, Lindblom states, an analysis must not target for the „synoptic/root" ideal but must seek to deploy them in the improvement of tactic to guide and direct: "something to be done, something to be studied and learned, and something can be successfully approximated".

The chief difference between 1959, and his latest version of 1979, „still muddling through" he trusts, selecting between „ill-considered, frequently accidental incompleteness on the one hand, and deliberately designed incompleteness on the other".

Disjointed Incrementalism:

The third kind of incremental analysis, which was claimed by Lindblom is „disjointed incrementalism". In the work „A Strategy of Decision" with David Braybrook, Lindblom introduced the idea of „disjointed incrementalism". He observes this as a procedure of decision making by which comparision takes place among policies that are slightly diverse from one another, and in which there is no „great goal" of view to be attained. Goals are fixed in terms of present resources and policymaking takes place by the „trial error" method. It can be called disjointed because the decisions do not matter to some kind of governor coordination. Lindblom places his work incrementalism in a continuum of knowledge and scale of change.

This disjointed incrementalism is regarded as an analytical tactic, which contains the following methods:

1. "The limitation of analyses for a few familiar alternatives

2. Interlocking values and policy goes with empirical analysis of problems

3. Focusing on ills to be remedied rather than on goals to be sought

4. Trail and error learning

5. Analyzing the limited number of options and their consequences

6. Fragmenting of analytical work to many partisan participants in policymaking".

Critical Evaluation:

Since, 1959 when Lindblom supported incremental decision making, there had been an obvious „volte-face" in his claim. In 1977 and 1979, Lindblom criticized the notion of pluralism, offered a radical attack on the business, and held that there is a want for severe radical change in an entire variety of policy zones and the entire world in terrible need of more than merely incremental change. But societies "seem incapable", except in emergencies, of acting more boldly than in increments". Nothing of such restraints on decision making and on the mode in which programs of the policy are scarcely made, he has severe suspicions as to the likelihood of any severe alteration.

The incremental method had been advanced and exposed to condemnation from several positions. Dror, yet, is not persuaded that the incremental model is either realistic or pleasing normative accounts of decision making. To Dror, this model is intensely conservative and is appropriate only in those conditions where policies are believed to be operational or are reasonable, where difficulties are fairly steady over time, and where there are resources accessible.

The instrumentalist's „method to policymaking is uncertain. As Lane stated, "It deductive power is constrained by the difficulty in specifying what an increment is, whilst its degree of confirmation is reduced by the typical occurrence of shift point in policy making which defy the interpretation of the incrementalist equations as stable linear growth models".

The vital distress of his work has been to discover the restraints that formed in decision-making in contemporary policy procedure. Incrementalism, it might be renowned, has not been a chief apprehensive of his writings sample as the connection between power, human information, and politics. Meant for him, "policymaking is a complexly interactive process without beginning or end".

Institutional Theory

Institutional Theory:

One of the oldest concerns of political science and public administration is the study of government institutions since political life generally revolves around them. These institutions include legislatures, executives, and the judiciary; and public policy is authoritatively formulated and executed by them. Traditionally, the institutional approach concentrates on describing the more formal and legal aspects of government institutions: their formal structure, legal powers, procedural rules, and functions. Formal relationships with other institutions might also be considered, such as legislative-executive relations. Usually, little was done to explain how institutions operated as opposed to how they were supposed to operate, to analyze public policies produced by the institutions, and to discover the relationships between institutional structure and public policies. Subsequently, social scientists turned their attention in teaching and research to the political processes within government or political institutions, concentrating on the behavior of participants in the process and on political realities rather than formalism. In the study of legislators, attention shifted from simply describing the legislature as an institution to analyzing and explaining its operation over time, from its static to its dynamic aspects. Thus, in the academic curriculum, the course on the legislature usually came to be about the legislative process. Institutionalism, with its emphasis on the formal or structural aspects of institutions, can nonetheless be usefully employed in policy analysis. An institution is, in part, a set of regularised patterns of human behavior that persist over time and perform some significant social function. It is their differing patterns of behavior that usually distinguish courts from legislatures, administrative agencies, and so on. These regularised patterns of behavior, which are usually called rules or structures, can affect decision-making and the content of public policy. Rules and structural arrangements are usually not neutral in their effects; rather, they tend to favor some interest in society over others, and some policy results over others. Using this approach in Nigeria at the national level, the primary institutions that would be the focus of policy analysis are invariably the legislative body, the executive, and the courts. In developing countries like Nigeria where we are still at a relatively low level of constitutional development, these institutions especially the first two, may take varying forms, depending on the regime in power. During the Second Republic when a democratically elected regime was in power the institutions were the National Assembly, the Federal Executive Council, and the Federal Courts. However, during military regimes, Supreme Military Council or Armed Forces Ruling Council was the legislative body, and the Council of Ministers was the executive. By this approach, it is taken for granted that the politics of Nigeria revolves around these institutions and therefore, an understanding of public policy in Nigeria requires a study of the constitution, operation, and relationships among these institutions.

In sum, institutional structures, arrangements, and procedures often have important consequences for the adoption and content of public policies. They provide part of the context for policy-making, which must be considered along with the more dynamic aspects of politics, such as political parties, groups, and public opinion in policy study. By itself, however, institutional theory can provide only partial explanations of policy.

This model studies the official structures and functions of government departments and institutions in an attempt to learn how public policy takes shape. It focuses on the organization chart of government. However, this model has shown little concern about the connections between a department and the public policy emanating from it. While the systems approach is dynamic and process-oriented, the institutionalist approach is more static and formalistic. As the behaviouralist movement took hold within political science during the 1950s and 1960s institutional studies of the policy process were gradually replaced by the empirical model. Based on the behaviouralist principles the empirical research makes an attempt to know how government institutions actually function. The empirical research makes use of experimental and quasi-experimental procedures to identify policy effects as precisely as possible. However, as Thomas Dye points out, the institutional approach can yield benefits to those concerned with how public policy takes shape (Naidu, 2006). It is more useful to view these models as complementary rather than competitive tools for the study of public policy-making as a process.

Etzioni's Mixed Scanning Method

Etzioni's Mixed Scanning Method:

Amitai Etzioni is another supporter of an altered usage of the rational model of policy analysis. Similar of Dror, he has reserved on extensive the disapproval of the rational method and has set forward a third kind of method which he trusts, and proposes a truthful model which evades the conservatism of the incrementalist location as expressed by Lindblom. Etzioni, states, his models mix scanning as,

"A rationalistic method to traditional making needs greater resources than decision-makers command. The incremental tactic which takes into account the restricted capability of actor fosters tradition which neglect basic societal innovations. Mixed scanning reduces the unrealistic aspects of rationalism by limiting the details needed in the fundamental decision and helps to overcome the conservative slant of incrementalism by exploring long run alternatives".

The notion Etzioni, about the mixed scanning is established from primary weather forecasting and observation technique. His notion has, however, located in the setting of his broader knowledgeable distresses and his work as a total. Later, the publication of his „mixed scanning", paper in 1967, Etzioni, published the last work on „The Active Society" in 1968. In 1990, he befitted most diligently related with communitarianism. Then the work, the active society continues, as may be the best overview to his notion of the policy analysis. Etzioni, trusts, that personal alteration is rooted in the combined performance of the community altering itself. He said that the object of public policy is eventually to encourage a society in which people are active in their communities and in which political action and intellectual replication would have a greater, more public position. That is to be attained over nurturing distinct and societal awareness and fresh stress on „symbolization" as contrasting to wealth. He states, "No man can set himself free without extending the same liberty to his fellow men and the transformation of the self is deeply rooted in the joint actio of a community transforming itself".

Therefore, Lindblom, does not abandon the usage of analysis it progresses society the stress on "community" which has been vital to his later writings, has hence, to be located in the background of his trust in the part of knowledge in carrying about a further exposed and more "authentic" public policy procedure.

For, Etzioni, an active society is one that includes the public in the analysis. Besides, in an active society, the knowledge elites- intellectual, expert, and politicians- must interact with the public in a method of shared realism challenge. Upgrading society, then, include both knowledge and moral measurement.

Etzioni, mixed scanning method tries to openly pool:

1. Extraordinary –order, important policy-making procedures which fixed elementary way, and

2. Incremental ones which make for essential decisions and work them out after they have been touched.

Etzioni, the notion of „mixed scanning „is a long way detached from Dror"s technocratic managerialism. For him, the mixed scanning method is an explanation of the actuality of decision-making tactics and it is also a model for healthy decision-making. It identifies that decision-makers have to reflect the costs of information since not entirety can be scanned. Therefore, policymakers must attempt to scan important parts completely and rationalistically and can focus other zones to an extra „truncated" evaluation.

Etzioni's Mixed Scanning Method:

Amitai Etzioni is another supporter of an altered usage of the rational model of policy analysis. Similar of Dror, he has reserved on extensive the disapproval of the rational method and has set forward a third kind of method which he trusts, and proposes a truthful model which evades the conservatism of the incrementalist location as expressed by Lindblom. Etzioni, states, his models mix scanning as,

"A rationalistic method to traditional making needs greater resources than decision-makers command. The incremental tactic which takes into account the restricted capability of actor fosters tradition which neglect basic societal innovations. Mixed scanning reduces the unrealistic aspects of rationalism by limiting the details needed in the fundamental decision and helps to overcome the conservative slant of incrementalism by exploring long run alternatives".

The notion Etzioni, about the mixed scanning is established from primary weather forecasting and observation technique. His notion has, however, located in the setting of his broader knowledgeable distresses and his work as a total. Later, the publication of his „mixed scanning", paper in 1967, Etzioni, published the last work on „The Active Society" in 1968. In 1990, he befitted most diligently related with communitarianism. Then the work, the active society continues, as may be the best overview to his notion of the policy analysis. Etzioni, trusts, that personal alteration is rooted in the combined performance of the community altering itself. He said that the object of public policy is eventually to encourage a society in which people are active in their communities and in which political action and intellectual replication would have a greater, more public position. That is to be attained over nurturing distinct and societal awareness and fresh stress on „symbolization" as contrasting to wealth. He states, "No man can set himself free without extending the same liberty to his fellow men and the transformation of the self is deeply rooted in the joint actio of a community transforming itself".

Therefore, Lindblom, does not abandon the usage of analysis it progresses society the stress on "community" which has been vital to his later writings, has hence, to be located in the background of his trust in the part of knowledge in carrying about a further exposed and more "authentic" public policy procedure.

For, Etzioni, an active society is one that includes the public in the analysis. Besides, in an active society, the knowledge elites- intellectual, expert, and politicians- must interact with the public in a method of shared realism challenge. Upgrading society, then, include both knowledge and moral measurement.

Etzioni, mixed scanning method tries to openly pool:

1. Extraordinary –order, important policy-making procedures which fixed elementary way, and

2. Incremental ones which make for essential decisions and work them out after they have been touched.

Etzioni, the notion of „mixed scanning „is a long way detached from Dror"s technocratic managerialism. For him, the mixed scanning method is an explanation of the actuality of decision-making tactics and it is also a model for healthy decision-making. It identifies that decision-makers have to reflect the costs of information since not entirety can be scanned. Therefore, policymakers must attempt to scan important parts completely and rationalistically and can focus other zones to an extra „truncated" evaluation.

System Model

System Model:

The work of David Easton, though not considered as basically concerned with „public policies", establishes a significant input to the development of policy methods. It gives a model of the political system that has an impact on the examination of policy tended to concentrate on the relationship between the policy formulation, policy results, and its broader atmosphere.

The important characteristic of this system is that, the policy procedure in relation to conversion from inputs into policy outcomes. The formulating of the policy procedure is considered as the „black box", which changes the demands of the society into policies. Easton in his, "Analysis of Political System" claims that the political system can be treated as the portion of the society which is involved in the „authoritative allocation of values". The system of political system view of Easton is as follows:

1. Inputs can be regarded as the social, economic, physical, and political harvests of the surroundings and they are established in the political organization in the procedure of demand and support.

2. Demands are the privileges that are created by the political system by persons and groups to change some features of the surroundings. Demands happen when persons or groups in reply to environmental situations,

perform to result in public policies.

3. The environment is any type of situation or happening defined as outside to the limitations of the political system.

4. The cohorts of the political system contain rules, customs, and laws which gives ground for the presence of a political community and authorities. These cohorts are rendered when persons or groups adopt the decisions or the laws. In any political system, they have organizations and employees involved in formulating the policy. These can be, legislature, executives, judges, and bureaucrats in the system who in fact interpret inputs into outputs.

5. The outputs, then are commanding principle sharing of the political system, and this sharing establishes public policy. The systems theory describes a public policy as "an output of the political system".

6. The main idea of the concept of „feedback" suggests that the public policies might be altering power on the surroundings and the demands created from there. And perhaps would have an effect on the character of the political system. Policy outputs perhaps create fresh demands and fresh followers, or withdrawal of the old followers for the system. These „feedbacks" have a significant part in creating the appropriate atmosphere for future policy

Restrictions of System Approach in Policy Analysis:

It is obvious that the systems theory is fruitful to help to know the policy-making procedure. According to Dye, „the value of the systems model to policy analysis rests on the query that it poses". The usefulness of the model to examine the public policy is limited having many reasons. It is claimed that this input-output seems to be too simplistic to perform as a useful help to know the policy formulating procedure. It is blamed for employing value-laden techniques of welfare economics which can be said as, „social welfare function".

The other criticism of this is the customary input-output model, which overlooks the fragmented nature of the „black box". The missing components of this system method are, "power, personnel and organizations" of public policymaking.

This model also overlooks a significant feature of the public policy procedure like, that the makers of the public policy have also substantial potential in persuading the surrounding inside which they perform. According to F. Cortes, The customary input-output model would observe the decision-making method as „facilitative" and value-free instead of „causative", that is, as a totally neutral structure. At the same time, J. Stonecash claimed that both the political and bureaucratic elite way the masses view, more than the masses natures the opinion of the leader. The concept of „with inputs" as opposed to inputs has been generated to explain this point.

Lastly, the extent to which the atmosphere including external and the internal is regarded to have an effect on the public policy-making procedure is influenced by the values and ideologies held by the decision-makers in the system. The values held by the policymakers are fundamentally assumed to be crucial in knowing the policy substitutes that are made. Easton"s input-output black box gives an overriding „macro" framework inside which the formulation of policy procedure will be outlined in the 1960s and 1970s.

Group Model

Group Model:

According to the group theory of politics, public policy is the product of the group struggle. What may be called public policy is the equilibrium reached in this group struggle at any given moment, and it represents a balance which the contending factions or groups constantly strive to win in their favor. Many public policies do reflect the activities of groups (Anderson, 1997). This means that this theory attempts to analyze how each of the various groups in society tries to influence public policy to its advantage at the policy formulation level. In other words, the central practice of this model is that interaction among groups is a critical ingredient in politics. Public policy is thus a temporary point of a compromise reached in the course of competition between mosaics of numerous interest groups with cross-cutting membership. The ability of the group that is favored at one point to sustain its gain depends on its power to counteract the powers of other groups that would make efforts to tilt decisions to their favor. Since the power to dominate policy decision is dependent on group solidarity and power, the dynamics of the policy process is expected to be more vibrant and fierce in plural societies than in homogenous ones. In such societies, the ability of a group to tilt the policy to its favor depends on a number of factors, prominent among which are:

- Wealth
- Organizational skill
- Leadership quality
- Bargaining skill
- Access to decision-makers or in Nigerian parlance "connection"
- A modicum of luck

This is one of the important theories in policy formulation, this public policy formulation model is demonstrated in the "hydraulic theory of politics" and this was stated by L. Harmon Zeigler and G. Wayne Peak. It was observed that the polity is observed as a method of forces and pressures, forceful against each other in the formulation of public policy. This theory initiates with the proposal that interaction among sets is the key point of politics. For an ordinary citizen, the pressure group is surely an essential network of influence and power. A group, whose associates have some mutual interest, presses its demands on the government. In this way, an assemblage becomes an imperative bond between the government and the individual. Truman stated about an interest group is "A shared attitude group that makes certain claims upon other groups in the society", and such a group becomes political, "If and when it makes a claim through or upon any of the institutions of government".

Used for the utmost portion an interest pursues to affect the policy decisions of the government. The set which impacts power is an overriding aspect of all democratic nations. Politics is really a tussle of power amongst dissimilar groups, while some are further possible than others to be worried about political power.

Forces for Group Equilibrium:

An advocate of the group theory claim that the public policy is the „equilibrium" which is firm by the group tussle or comparative impact of any interest groups. The impact of the group is resolute by its number, wealth, and strength of the organization, leadership, access to the decision-makers, and inside unity. The public policy will change in the way wanted by the group which has grown more influence. From the group theory lookout, and Latham, stated about public policy, "What may be called public policy is actually the equilibrium reached in the group struggle at any given moment, and it represents a balance which the contending factions or groups constantly strive to tip in their favor...the legislature referees the group struggle, ratifies the victories of the successful coalition and records the terms of the surrenders, compromises, and conquests in the form of statutes".

The vital point of group theory is political action in relation to the group tussle. Policy formulators in this theory are observed as answering to group forces (negotiating and compromising) amongst opposing the demands of influential groups. Politicians and the political parties „effort to practice a mainstream coalition of groups. In doing so, they may choose the groups, which have varied interests, to form a majority coalition. The group theory grip that, numerous forces back to uphold equilibrium in the total interest group. Firstly, a big dormant group in the society backs the constitutional system of the nation. Secondly, overlying group membership aids to uphold the equilibrium by stopping any one group from violating the constitutional method and prevalent standards. The point is that the persons belonging to further than one group curb the demands of the groups who should evade upsetting members of other group associations. And thirdly, equilibrium outcomes from group competition. The influence of one group is tested by the influence of other rival groups.

Focus in Groupthink Theory:

The research on the influence of groups on persons has revealed how influential the group can be in misrepresenting rulings and decision-making. Persons in groups are under pressure to follow group standards and insight into information. But the cohesiveness of a group is the main issue in the attainment of jobs. In the setting, Janis has advocated groupthink theory; "the physiological drive for consensus in cohesive decision-making groups".

Faults in the Group-Decision Making:

Janis claims that because the associates of a group are faithful to a group's lookout accord shades decision-makers to the certainties. A great level of examination into the „challenger" disaster of 1986, did plug out the five types of mistakes in NASA"s decision-making process. And they are

1. Apparent pressure to crop a wanted approval (some members initially opposed to the launch):

2. An obvious reluctance to intrude upon supposed roles

3. A doubtful design of reasoning amongst main managers

4. An unclear use of language 5. Failure to ask vital questions.

Measures for Combating the Groupthink Process:

From the instances of the group decision with two case studies of the Marshall Plan and the Cuban missile crisis Janis, derived a sum of measures to fight the groupthink decision making procedure and they are as follows:

1. Leader has a role in boosting serious assessment in all followers and the manifestation of suspicions and protests

2. Main leaders state partiality when handover policy planning and analysis

3. Decision making necessity be led through the setting up of numerous policy planning and assessment groups

4. Since time-to-time the group that brands the policy should separate into subgroups and see under dissimilar chairpersons

5. Associates of the policy formulating groups must deliberate with reliable members" outer group 6. Experts and other not from the policy making group must come and in and be inspire to challenge the group.

7. Substitutes must be assessed at the very meeting

8. If the issues of policy are tangled a rival nation or organization, much of the time should be given to surveying the signals and intension of opposition

9. After coming to the assumption a second meeting must be summoned to permit the expression of doubts

Criticism of Groupthink Theory:

The important objections to the groupthink theory are as follows:

1 .The shortages of the case study procedure for the hypothesis examination, the menace of choosy care to indicate and entice to apt untidy historical truths into essential theoretical groups.

2. The doubtfully flawless connection among reliability of procedure and the goodness of result (the risk of hindsight)

3. The all or nothing assignment of decision making affairs into the groupthink and watchful classes (the threat of moderating variance inside a grouping and of overstating variance between groupings)

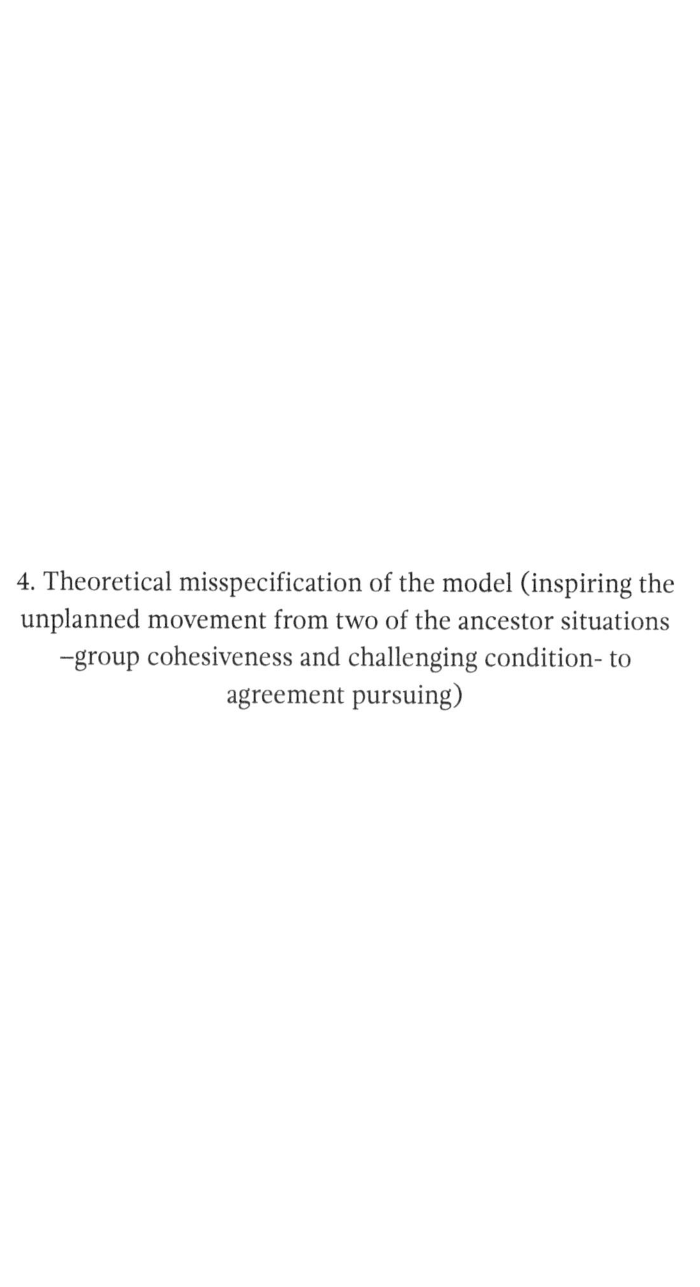

4. Theoretical misspecification of the model (inspiring the unplanned movement from two of the ancestor situations –group cohesiveness and challenging condition- to agreement pursuing)

Elite Model

Elite Model:

The elite theory of public policy procedure is grounded on the plan that power is focused on the small number of people. According to this theory, Public policy formulation is a procedure that performs according to the benefits of the elites, the theory grips that, in the actual world, there are some people at the top with the power and the mass without power at the bottom. The theory deal with that the elite who has more money and these members have common values, education power, and rules the masses who are unconcerned in ill-informed about the public policy. In the surrounding, the elite will have an impact on the mass views on the issues of the policy more than the impact of the masses influence the elite opinions.

In this procedure, the policy flows downward from the elite to the mass. According to Thomas R. dye and Harmon Zeigler, who stated about public policy is, „the preferences and values of the governing elite".

In fact, the theory has its origins in the work of Mosca and Pareto, who are Italian theorists, who claimed that dissimilar to Marx, elitism is unavoidable and that classless society is a myth. After that, Mosca altered his opinion and claimed that democracy can be opined as a system of politics in which the elite contest for the vote of the people so as to obtain legality for the elite rule.

Portrayal on the notions of Mosca, Robert Michels in a study of political parties claimed that there was an iron law of oligarchy which functioned in organizations.

Propositions of Elitism:

The important propositions of the elite theory are as follows:

1. The society is separated into elite who actually rules and have the power to decide on the public policy and the masses are ruled by them and do not have any power to decide on public policy.

2. These elites share common values and contain money, education, and power than the masses who actually are apathetic and ill-informed. These elite associates are drawn excessively from the developed socio-economic sections of society.

3. Public policy does not reproduce the demands of the masses, but instead the likings and values of the ruling elite.

4. The ground of elites, who share consensus on the primary values of the social structure, is the sanctity of private property, restricted government, and personal freedom.

5. These elites form opinions of the masses on policy issues more than the masses shape elite opinion.

Lasswell and Mills' Contribution to Elitism:

In the development of elite theory the contribution of Lasswell cannot be overlooked, he opined that the "the study of politics is the study of influence and the influential…The influential are those who get the most of what there is to get…those who get the most are elite, the rest are mass".

Lasswell agreed to the notion of Pareto, and he claimed that different „skill groups" had arisen from the class tussle in the democracy. These skill groups contain those skilled in the practice of violence, those with communication publicity skills, those with business and commercial skills, technocrats, who have exceptional technical skills, and bureaucrats with administrative skills. He was apprehensive that the mixture of these two new elites pretended a risky menace to democracy and elevated the scene of the development of the „garrison-state" in which military, bureaucratic and technocratic elites govern. Lasswell said policy science will have a significant role in improving democracy by looking to promote an extensive distribution and pluralism of power.

Implications of the Elite Theory:

This elite theory identifies the drive of elite mass struggle, it has definite implications to know the policy analysis. Michels claimed that there were iron laws of the oligarchy which operated in organizations. The organizational elites generate their own interests and aims which are different from those masses.

CHAPTER THREE

THE PROCESS OF PUBLIC POLICY FORMULATION

THE PROCESS OF PUBLIC POLICY FORMULATION

Public policy involves an interactive and dynamic process and is never a one-time event. In most cases, public policy deals with the rules and directives associated. It comprises a sub-policy that includes the exact details about the policy, together with the concerned implementation techniques.

There are five main steps involved in the public policy process include following:

- Identification of the Problem
- Formulation of Policy
- Adaption of Policy
- Implementation of Policy
- Evaluation of Policy

In a nutshell, formulating, implementing, and following public policies helps to regulate and rectify the operations of governance. Every institution needs to have its own set of rules and regulations public Policy, and laws to hold everything in place.

Policy formulation may begin at the top of an organization or at the bottom or at the middle levels of management. Whatever the starting point, the entire organization becomes involved directly or indirectly. Policies beginning at the top levels arise out of needs perceived by top executives. Such needs which affect the entire organization must be met so that the organization may work satisfactorily and efficiently to achieve the desired ends.

Once a policy is established at the top, it becomes the guide for supporting policies that may emanate from successively lower levels. Policy not only originates at the top and flows downward, but also may originate at or near the bottom and flow upward in an organization. The extent to which this occurs depends largely on the extent to which these levels are allowed and encouraged to express their opinions.

Policy formulation actually requires a master hand. Martin Starr suggests three rules for formulating commonly used policies. These are:-

1. strive for equilibrium, not optimization:

2. Use ethics and social values as a basis and stay away from consideration of larger systems and

3. call on accepted tradition and avoid innovations.

According to Starr effective policies are those that are supported by the group over a long enough period to become accepted practice.

Charles E. Lindblom uses the concept of the policymaking process to achieve a focus of inquiry into certain aspects of political processes. According to him a policy sometimes occurs as a result of a political compromise among policymakers. Sometimes policies, spring from new opportunities and not from problems at all, And sometimes policies are not decided upon but nevertheless "happen". Lindblom views policy making as an extremely complex analytical and political process to which there is no beginning or end, and the boundaries of which are most uncertain.

Policy Implementation

Once a policy decision has been taken by the Government, approved by the Cabinet, and expressed in the form of a law passed by the Parliament or the State Legislature concerned or through the promulgation of an ordinance by the President of India or the Governor of a State as the case may be when the Parliament or the State Legislature concerned are not in session, it is absolutely essential that the implementation of the policy is ensured to achieve the objective, purpose or goal for which the policy decision has been taken. For this, a proper mechanism has to be provided. It is mainly the executive comprising bureaucrats, officers, and officials of the Government who are entrusted with the task of execution or implementation of the policy. They are responsible to the Minister in Incharge of the Ministry/Department concerned for effective implementation of the policy of the government in the respective ministries/Departments. The bureaucracy is expected to be committed to performing their duties efficiently, honestly, devotedly, and dedicatedly to serve the people. They monitor the progress of the implementation of the policy through proper liaison with their functionaries operating at the headquarters or in the field by paying regular visits to the places of work, listening to the grievances of the clientele concerned regarding the availability of benefits which were to accrue to them through the policy announcements, by taking appropriate action, to get the appropriations sanctioned for the programs released well in time, to ensure the supply of the material required for a particular project, to take the erring officials to task, to motivate the functionaries, to perform their duties, to take the public into confidence and to secure their active participation in the implementation of the policy meant for their benefit and welfare. Above all, there should have a political will to get the policies executed which are supposed to be people-oriented, action-oriented, and result-oriented.

Late Prime Minister Rajiv Gandhi was very much concerned about the proper implementation of government policies. He was constrained to observe those objectives to be achieved by various policies that had failed to be realized. In his words, only fifteen paise out of a rupee granted for development and welfare of the people concerned reached the beneficiaries and the rest of it was appropriated by the middlemen and government officials. He was regularly monitored. He had created a Department of Programme Implementation in 1985 which was headed by a Cabinet Minister or Minister of State and where the Secretary was an Indian Administrative officer. The Department was required to submit an annual report on its work to the Parliament. But unfortunately, the Department has not been able to achieve the desired objective of properly monitoring the implementation of various programs for lack of cooperation by the policy implementing organizations. The Minister concerned and the Bureaucrat Secretary have also not been enthusiastic in their respective assignments as they feel that the task of monitoring is not that challenging or rewarding as the field of action. And as mentioned earlier, another important cause of unsatisfactory implementation of government policies has been the absence of involvement of people in the formulation and implementation of policies. Consequently, some of the government policies have remained on paper only and confined to files without achieving even partially the objectives for the attainment of which they were formulated. For instance, our population control policy for the execution of which thousands of crores of rupees have been spent has not been successful. On the contrary, there has been a population explosion raising our population to one thousand million approximately, making it number two in terms of population with China occupying the first position which is likely to be taken up by us in the next decade if we fail to control our birthrate. That has been the case with our food policy also. Despite our having adequate buffer stocks of food stuff, the prices of commodities of daily use have been skyrocketing and responsible for marring the fate of governments in the states where elections had been held in November 1998.

Among the various causes for the unsatisfactory implementation of our public policies, the most conspicuous is said to be lack of consistency, inadequate political sense of civil servants, limited political competence, inadequate organizational capability, and absence of strong public policy pressure groups. In addition, communalism, regionalism, casteism, terrorism, people's apathy and infighting within various political parties, factionalism, and groups have also been responsible for poor policy implementation. It is desirable that cooperation and coordination among different governmental organizations implementing certain policies should be ensured and people should be involved in the process of policy formulation and execution so that the right policies are framed and these are rightly implemented.

Policy Evaluation

It is extremely important that Public Policies should be properly evaluated and appraised to determine their impact to ascertain how far they have been successful in achieving the objectives or goals for which they were formulated and implemented, to find out what factors have contributed to their acceptance, and approval by the society and what causes have been responsible for their disapproval or rejection by the people and what modifications or changes should be brought about in them to ensure their validity, reasonableness and what bottlenecks if any, should be removed to achieve the desired purposes and objectives. There are many organizations, institutions, and agencies involved in the task of evaluation of policies some of which may be mentioned as follows:

(i) Planning Commission which is the fountainhead of many policies has a plan-evaluation organization to evaluate its policies and programs. It also undertakes a midterm review of the ongoing plans. The states have their State Planning Boards which also evaluate periodically their plans and programmes.

(i) Parliamentary Committees, such as Public Accounts Committees, Estimates Committee and Committee on Public Undertakings, in their reports presented to the Parliament devote substantial part to evaluation of the executing of policies and make suggestions and recommendations for removing defects and discrepancies in them and to evolve new policies to make them more effective.

(iii) The Committees comprising members of Parliament are attached to every Ministry/Department. Their meetings are convened by the Ministers concerned where they evaluate the public policies and exchange views and ideas to reach a consensus for the adoption of the right policies.

(iv) The Comptroller and Auditor General of India in his annual report submitted to the Parliament critically evaluates the government policies and elaborates how far certain policies have not been able to achieve the designated objectives and what modifications should be undertaken to ensure the effectiveness of policy formulation and implementation and the utilization of funds provided for various programs wisely and economically for the purposes only for which they have been appropriated. The report also points out the irregularities and wastage committed to the execution of policies and recommends to the government to take suitable action against the authorities at fault.

(v) Public Policies are evaluated constantly by the political parties. They express their views on govt, policies for public consumption through the platform, press, and electronic media, and their election manifestoes include criticism of the wrong policies being pursued by the existing government and the steps they propose to take to rectify them and usher in new policies for the wellbeing and welfare of the society.

(vi) Non-Government Organisations (N.G.O's.), Voluntary Organisations and Associations are also engaged in the evaluation of public policies. For instance, Help-Age India and Care-Age India evaluate the Govt. policies concerning senior citizens and old age people and suggest to the governments what policies shall be adopted for providing security economic, health, and emotional, of the old people.

(vii) Media Public Policies are evaluated by the media also. Various pronouncements of government policies are mentioned in the newspapers and broadcast by Radio and televisions and the public reaction to these policies both favorable and unfavorable by individuals or groups are reported with regard to their evaluation by the concerned sections of society.

(viii) Editorials Public Policies are evaluated by the editors of important newspapers in the Editorials with comments on their pros and cons. Every day editorials appear in various newspapers on one public policy or the other. Our nuclear policy which was made a target of criticism by vested interests inside and outside the country after the Pokhran II Nuclear Explosion in May 1998 was vehemently defended in the editorials and international opinion was brought around our justification for going nuclear.

(ix) Seminars and Conferences are also organized to assess the impact of certain policies. Our foreign policy, defense policy, etc. have been discussed and evaluated at various national and international seminars and conferences to impress upon the world community our genuine concerns for peace and cooperation among various countries for the progress and prosperity of their people.

(x) Articles in Journals Public Policies have been the theme and focus of articles contributed by distinguished academicians, scholars, and specialists for publication in some journals of repute. The Indian Journal of Public Administration, the Quarterly Journal of Indian Institute of Public Administration New Delhi has published some illuminating articles on public policy formulation, implementation, and evaluation in some of its issues. A few books have also been published on the subject for the benefit of students of Political Science, Public Administration and Economics, and the general public.

(xi) Research Institutes - Some Research Institutes are also engaged in the task of evaluation of public policies. To mention a few of these, the Centre for Policy Research examines the effectiveness of various public policies. The Indian Defence Research Institute concentrates on the evaluation of defense policies and our defense preparedness. The Institute of Foreign Trade looks into the effectiveness of the commercial policies of the government.

(xii) The Reserve Bank of India evaluates the monetary and fiscal policies of the government and presents its view in its review on the currency and finance situation of the country. Similarly, the Institute of Public Finance and Policy evaluates the policy with regard to the public finances of the country.

(xiii) International and Regional Institutions, Commonwealth Secretariat as also the World Bank, International Monetary Fund, and other International Agencies like WHO, UNICEF, ILO, and UNESCO evaluate our policies relating to their concerned fields in their annual reports.

(xiv) Experts' views: Experts and Specialists in various fields make a significant contribution to the evaluation of public policies by examining them dispassionately. Sometimes the government solicits their opinions on various policies and seeks their advice for the right policy decisions. Prime Minister Shri Atal Bihari Vajpayee has sought a meeting with Prof. Amitya Sen who has been awarded the Nobel Prize for his Welfare Economics to know about his views and opinions for our policies on economic growth, development, and welfare of poor sections of society.

(xv) Role of Universities: The Universities also evaluate and appraise the public policies through research on various policies such as Reservation Policy for Scheduled Castes, Scheduled Tribes, and other backward classes. Empowerment of Women, Panchayati Raj institutions, Urban local bodies, Rural Development Programmes, etc., undertaken by the Postgraduate students in their dissertations and thesis for M-Phil, Ph.D. and Post-doctoral Degrees.

The role of various organizations, institutions, and agencies in the evaluation of public policies is indeed encouraging and commendable. But it is regrettable that their evaluation findings and suggestions made for the formulation of the right policies and ensuring their effective implementation are not given due consideration and proper application by the government. It is desirable and advisable that the evaluation reports of the public policies should be accorded due weightage in the formulation and implementation of policies to serve the interests of the country and its people in the best possible manner.

CHAPTER FOUR

PARTICIPANTS IN PUBLIC POLICY FORMULATION

PARTICIPANTS IN PUBLIC POLICY FORMULATION

Across the globe and from one country to the other, societies are bedeviled by myriads of problems. Indeed, such problems span all areas of human endeavors- political, socio-economic, cultural, environmental, religious, and security to mention a few. Over the years, human beings, through their various governments, engage one major and potent instrument called "policy" to address and solve problems of societies and issues that are of public concern. The policy process is an intricate process involving certain actors in government as well as those outside government (who find relevance in the existence of government). These actors or participants are crucial and influential in the sub-processes of policy initiation, choices, formulation, implementation, and evaluation.

Unofficial Policymakers:

Unofficial policymakers do not occupy formal public positions or political offices. They are not in government but they derive their relevance and policy-making roles from the government and the official policymakers. Mainly, they harness their interests and demands, harmonize them and influence official policymakers to factor them into the policymaking process.

Official Policymakers:

According to Anderson, the official policymakers are those who possess the legal authority to engage in the formulation of public policy. Those involved in this category are the legislators, the executive, the administrators, and the judiciary. Each of them performs policy-making responsibilities in a different way from the others. They are governmental actors who occupy formal public positions and political offices and serve as actual policymakers. Official policymakers are in turn categorized by Anderson (1979) and Egonmwan (1991) into (i) primary policymakers; and (ii) supplementary policymakers. The primary policymakers are constitutionally empowered to engage in the formulation of policies. It is their constitutional assignment and responsibility. Consequently, they need not depend upon other governmental agencies or units, or structures to perform their policy-making roles. In Nigeria, for example, they are members of the National Assembly (the Senate and the House of Representatives) and states' Houses of Assembly. In Nigeria's current democratic dispensation, other significant primary policymakers include the president, his aides, administrators, and judges. They, as well, contribute as supplementary policymakers. The supplementary policymakers, expectedly, receive their authority to act in the policy-making process from the primary policymakers such as the National Assembly in Nigeria. They are expected to be responsive to the interests and requests of the National Assembly. Examples of supplementary policymakers are persons, agencies, or bodies that need authority from others in order to act as they are dependent on, or are controlled by others. They include ministries, departments, and other governmental agencies that initiate policies and push for them.

There are politicians in the policy-making process and these refer to all elected political office holders and those who occupy political posts/offices. They include the president (as the chief executive), his political aides and advisers, legislators in the National Assembly (the Senate and the House of Representatives), and members of the states' Houses of Assembly.

CHAPTER FIVE

BIBILOGRAPHY

- Anderson, James E. Public Policymaking, 7th ed. Cengage Learning, 2011.
- Abdulsami, I. (1987). The Concept and Process of Public Policy. A paper presented at the national workshop for chief nursing officers, in Zaria, Wednesday 3rd June 1987.
- Anderson, J.E.(1997). Public Policy-Making: An Introduction 3rd ed. Boston: Houghton Mifflin Company.
- Brewer, Garry and Peter DeLeon (1983). The Foundations of Policy Analysis, Pacific Grove: Brooks/ Cole.
- Bush, GW (2001). State of the Union address, 27 February. Available online.
- Braybrooke, D. &Lindblom, E. (1964).A Strategy of Decisions. Free Press of Glencoe, New York.
- Carter, James (1977). Speech, 18 April. American Experience, PBS. Available online.
- Denhardt, Robert and Joseph Grubbs (2003). Public Administration: an action orientation. Belmont, CA: Thomson.
- Dlakwa, H.D. (2014). Concepts and Models in Public Policy Formulation and Analysis. Kaduna:

PylamakServicies Ltd Nigeria.

- Downs, A. (1957). An Economic Theory of Democracy. New York: Harper and Row
- Dye, T.R & Zeigler, L.H. (1990).The Irony of Democracy. 8 edition. Monterey, Califf: Books/Cole
- Hayes, M.T. (1992). Incrementalism and Public Policy. New York: Longman.
- Henry, N. (2004). Public Administration and Public Affairs. New Delhi: Prentice Hall.
- Latham,E. (1965). The Group Basis of Politics, New York: Octagon Books
- Mitchell, W.C. (1982). Textbook Public Choice: A Review Essay. Public Choice, XXVIII
- Mosca, G. (1939). The Ruling Class, (Translated by Hannah D. Kahn), New York: McGraw-Hill Book Company.
- Obi, E.A, Nwachukwu, C.L. and Obiora, A.C. (2008).Public Policy Analysis and Decision Making. Onitsha: Bookpoint Educational Ltd.
- Patton, Carl and David Sawicki (1993). Basic Methods of Policy Analysis and Planning. Englewood Cliffs, NJ: Prentice Hall.
- Peters, B. Guy (1992). "The policy process: an institutionalist perspective." Canadian Public Administration 35(2).
- Stone, Deborah (2002). Policy Paradox. New York: W.W. Norton.
- Simon, H.A. (1957). Administrative Behaviour: A Study of Decision-Making Processes in Administrative Organisation. New York: The Macmillian Company.
- Viana, Ana Luiza (1996). "Abordagens metodológicas em políticas públicas," in Revista da Administração Pública, 30(2): 5-43.

- Cochran, CLARKE E., et al. American Public Policy: An Introduction, 1Oth ed. Belmont, CA: Wadsworth, Cengage Learning, 2011.
- Dunn, WILLIAM N. Public Policy Analysis, 4th ed. New York: Pearson Michael 2008. KRAFT, Michael E., and Scott R. FuRLONG.
- Public Policy: Politics, Analysis, and Alternatives, 3rd ed. Washington, DC: CQ PrGuy, 2009.
- PETERS, B. Guy. American Public Policy: Promise and Performance, 8th ed. Washington, DC: CQ Press, 2009.
- Rushefskey, Mark E. Public Policy in the United States, 4th ed. Armonk, NY: M. E. Sharpe, 2008. WEINER, DAVID and ALDEN R. VINING.
- Policy Analysis: Concepts and Practice, 5th ed. New York: Longman, 2011.
- Weischler, L.F. Methodological Individualism in Politics. Public Administration Review, XL III, May/June 1982.
- Wildavsky, Aaron. Speaking Truth to Power. New York: John Wiley, 1979.

www.ingramcontent.com/pod-product-compliance
Lightning Source LLC
Chambersburg PA
CBHW021116130726
47988CB00003B/1041